This Book is dedicated to:

Avery K

Claire E

Kinley E

Jonah R

I hope you enjoy coloring the following pages as much as i enjoyed designing them. Please feel free to email me to relate what you liked about the designs and what kind of designs you want to see in the next book.

God Bless You and your family,

Debbie

coloringbookelegance@yahoo.com

Created by Debbie Wilfong Appleby

Contributions made by Andrea Yingling

coloringbookelegance.com

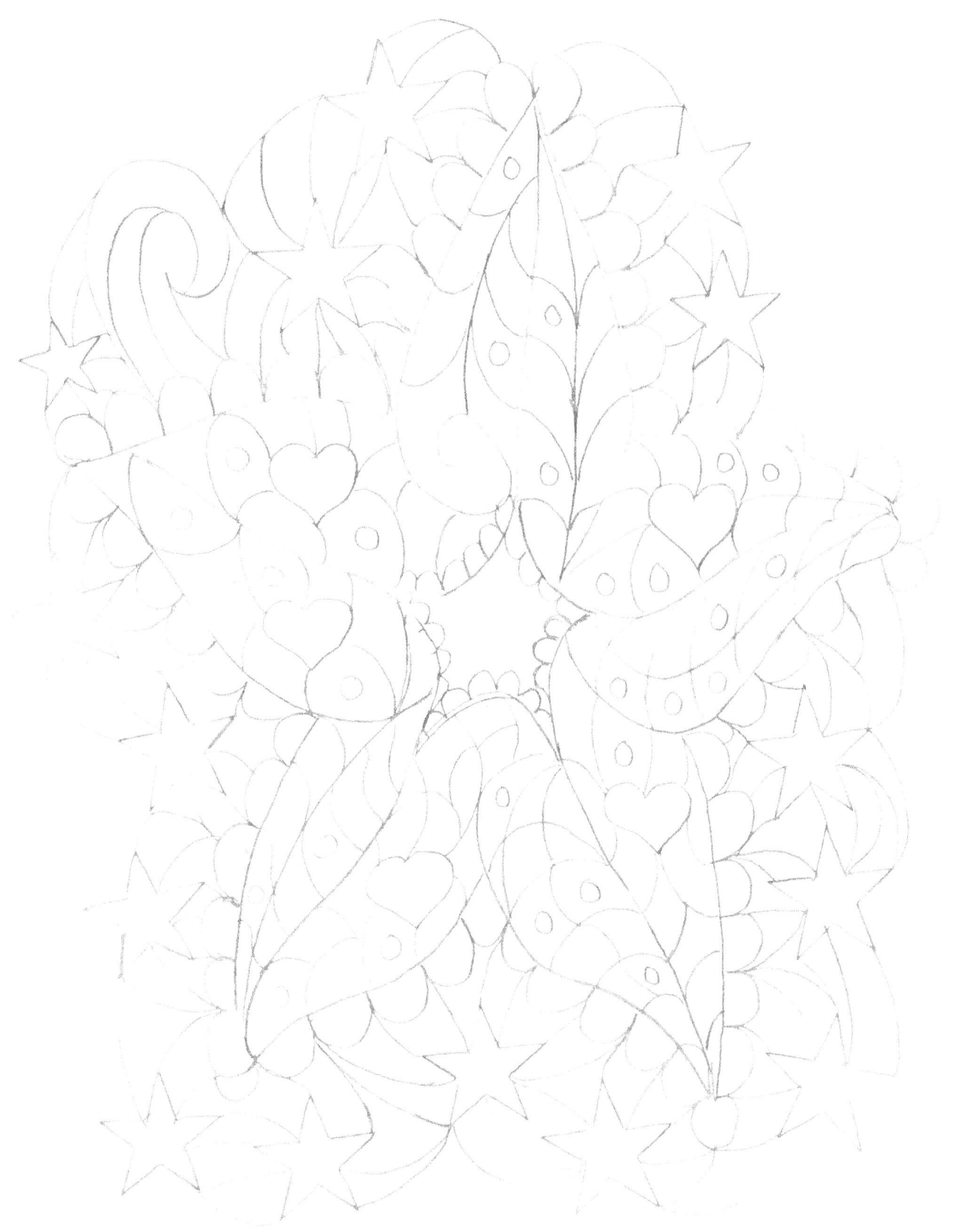

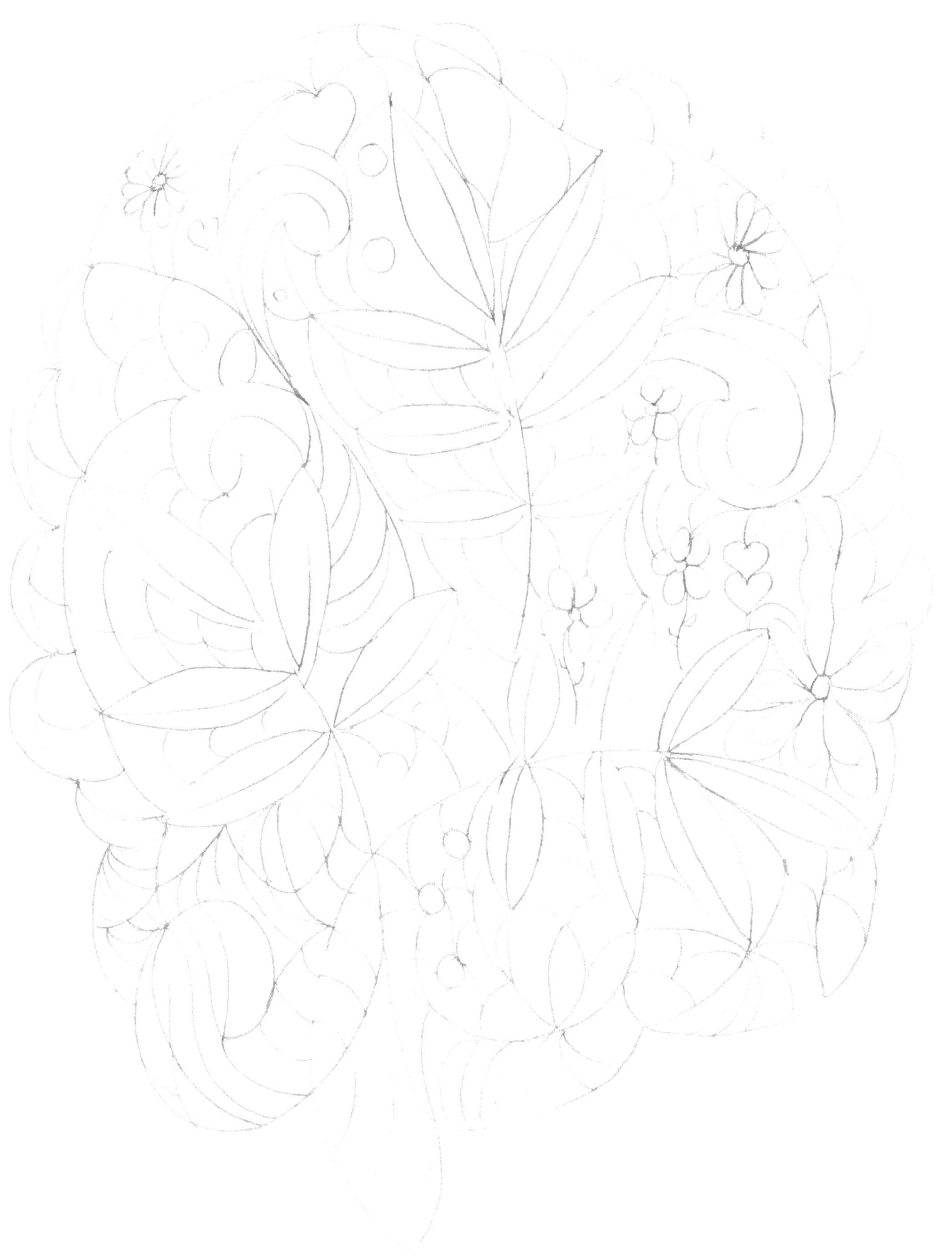

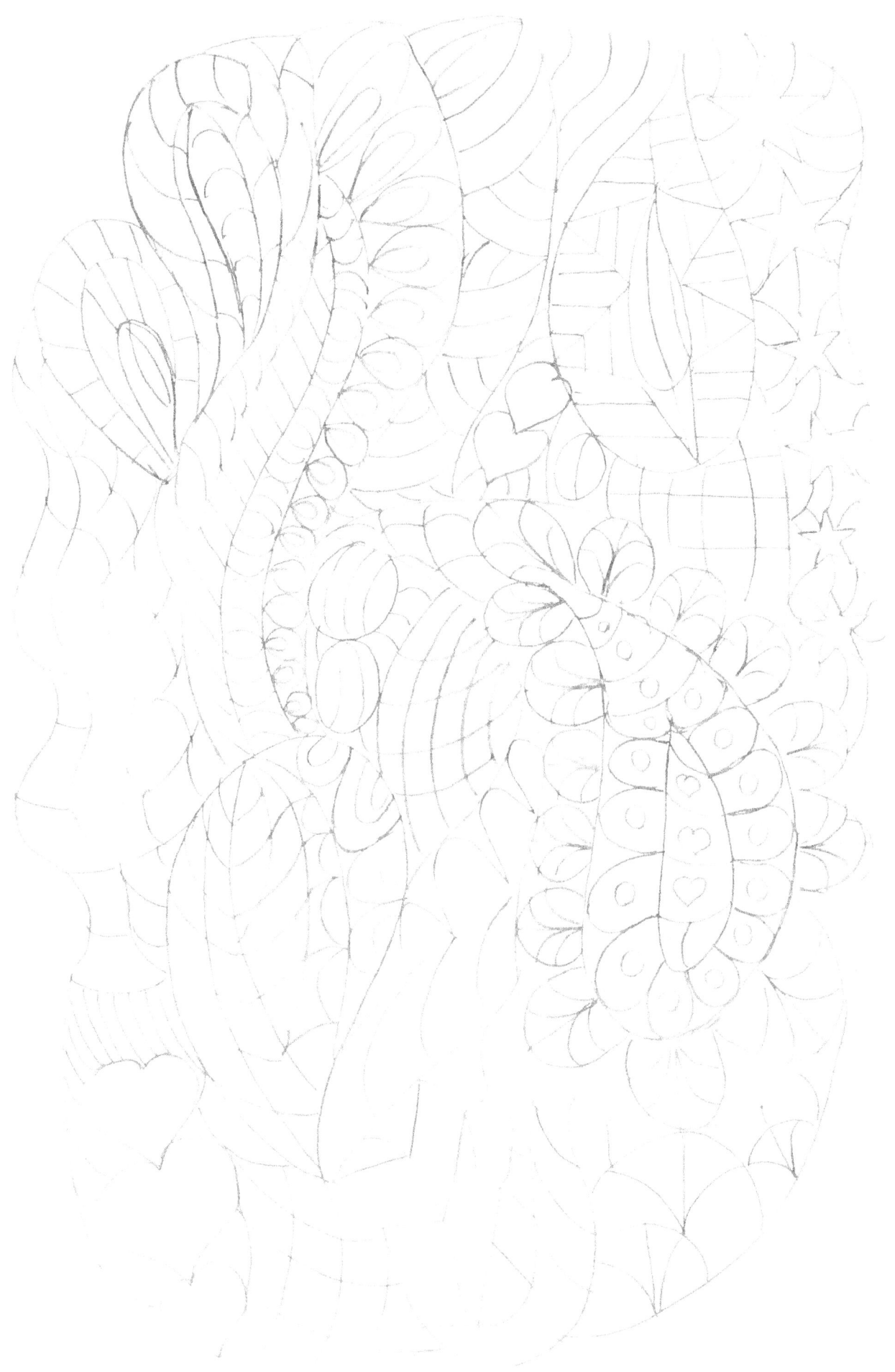

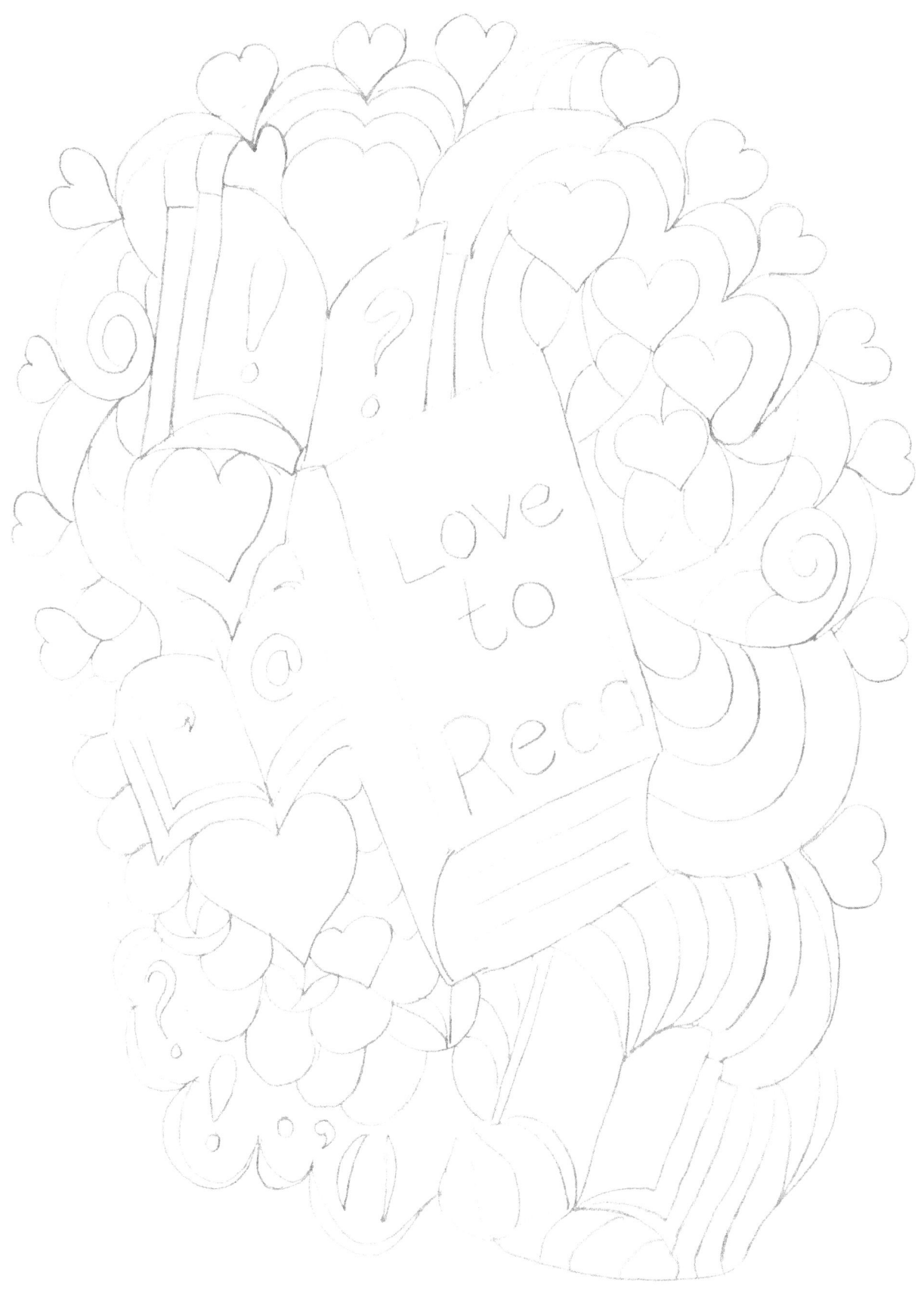

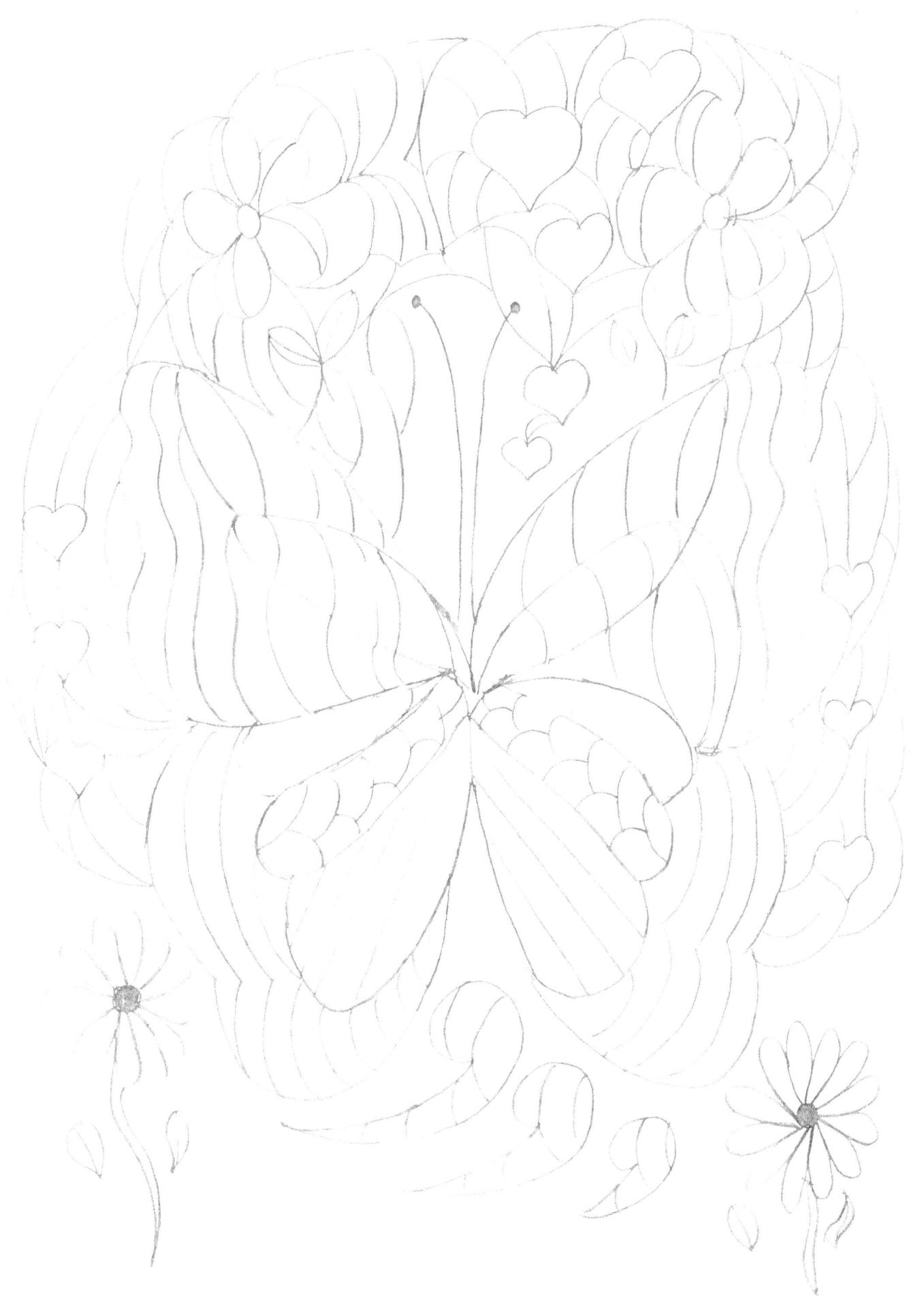

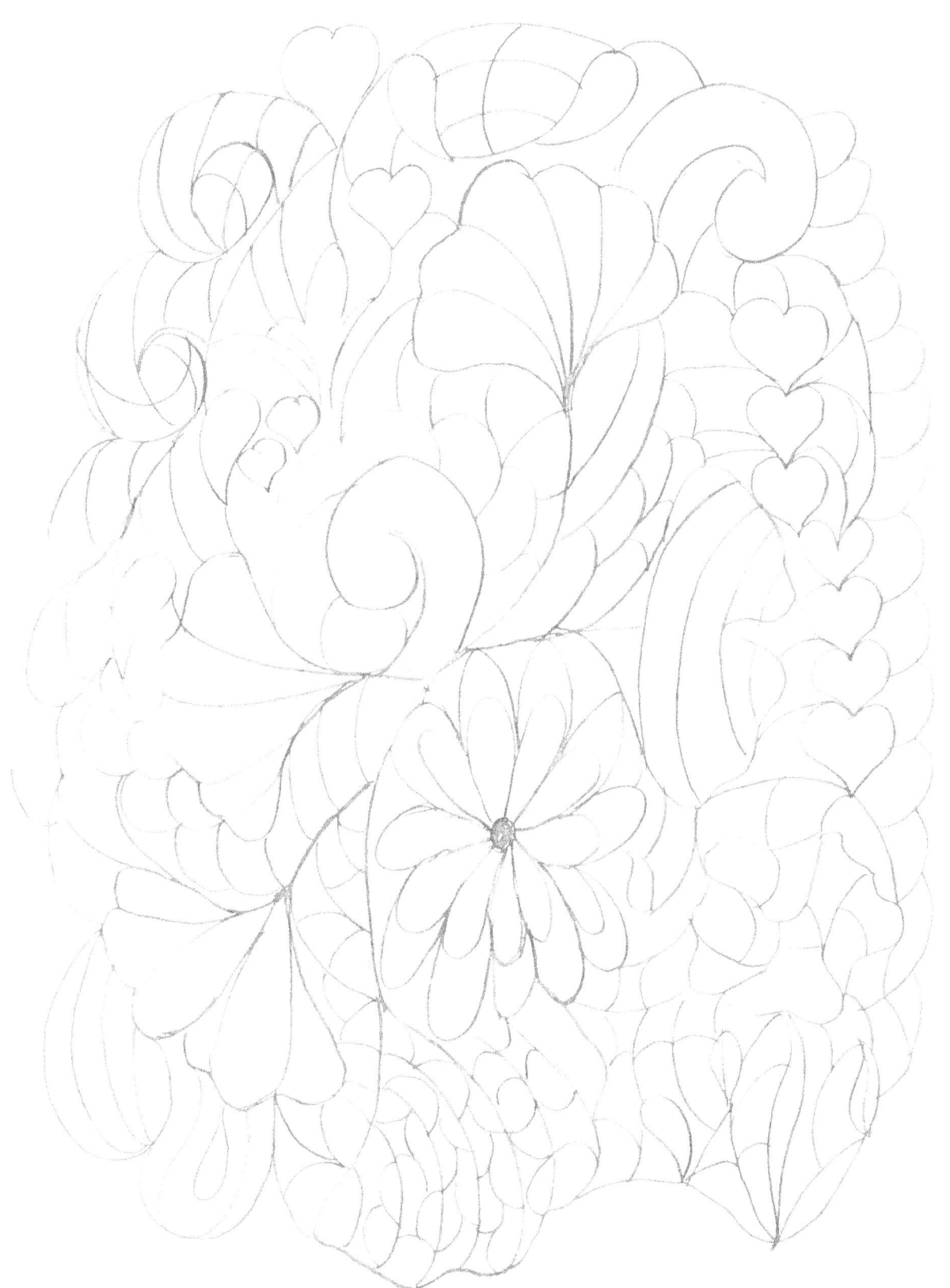

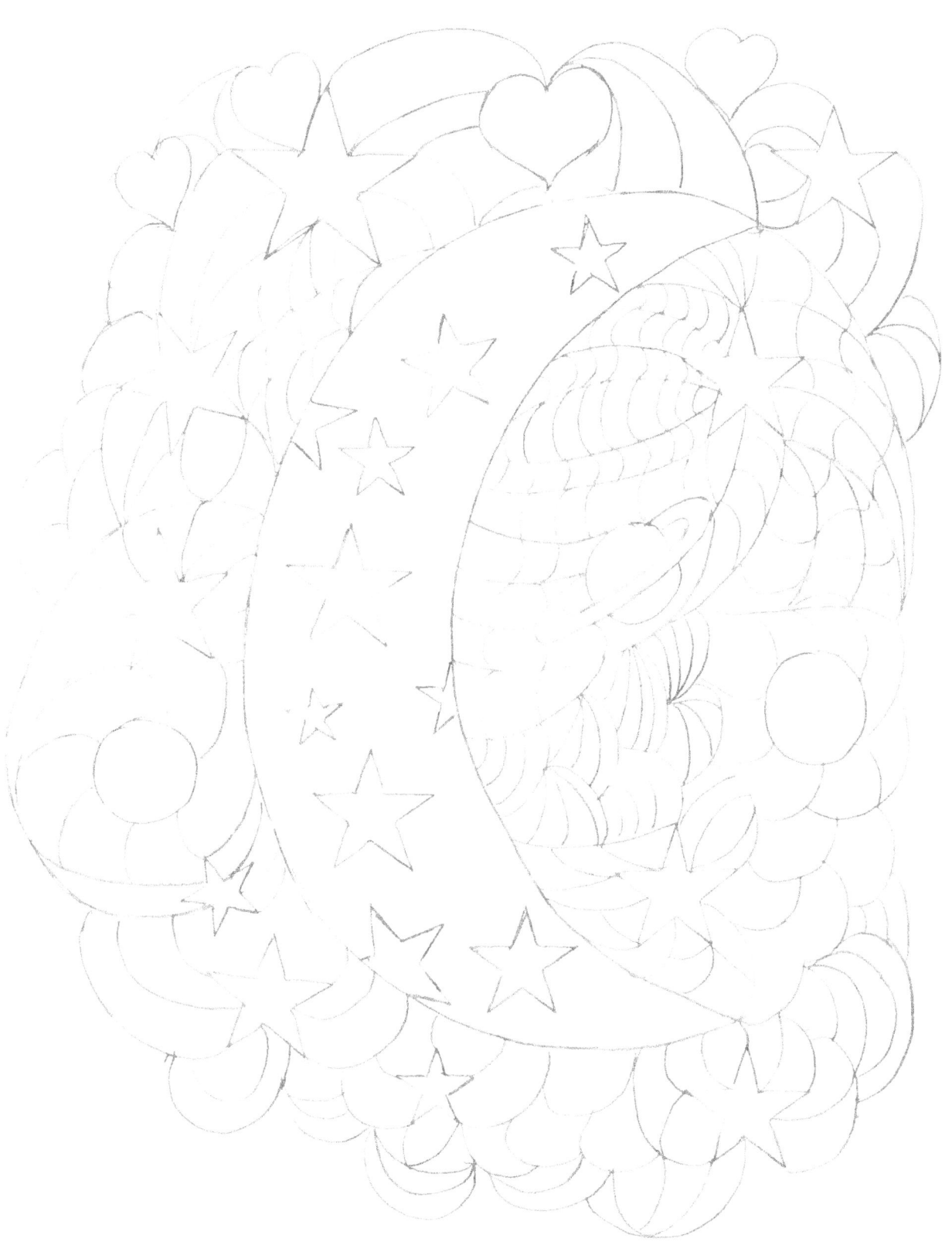

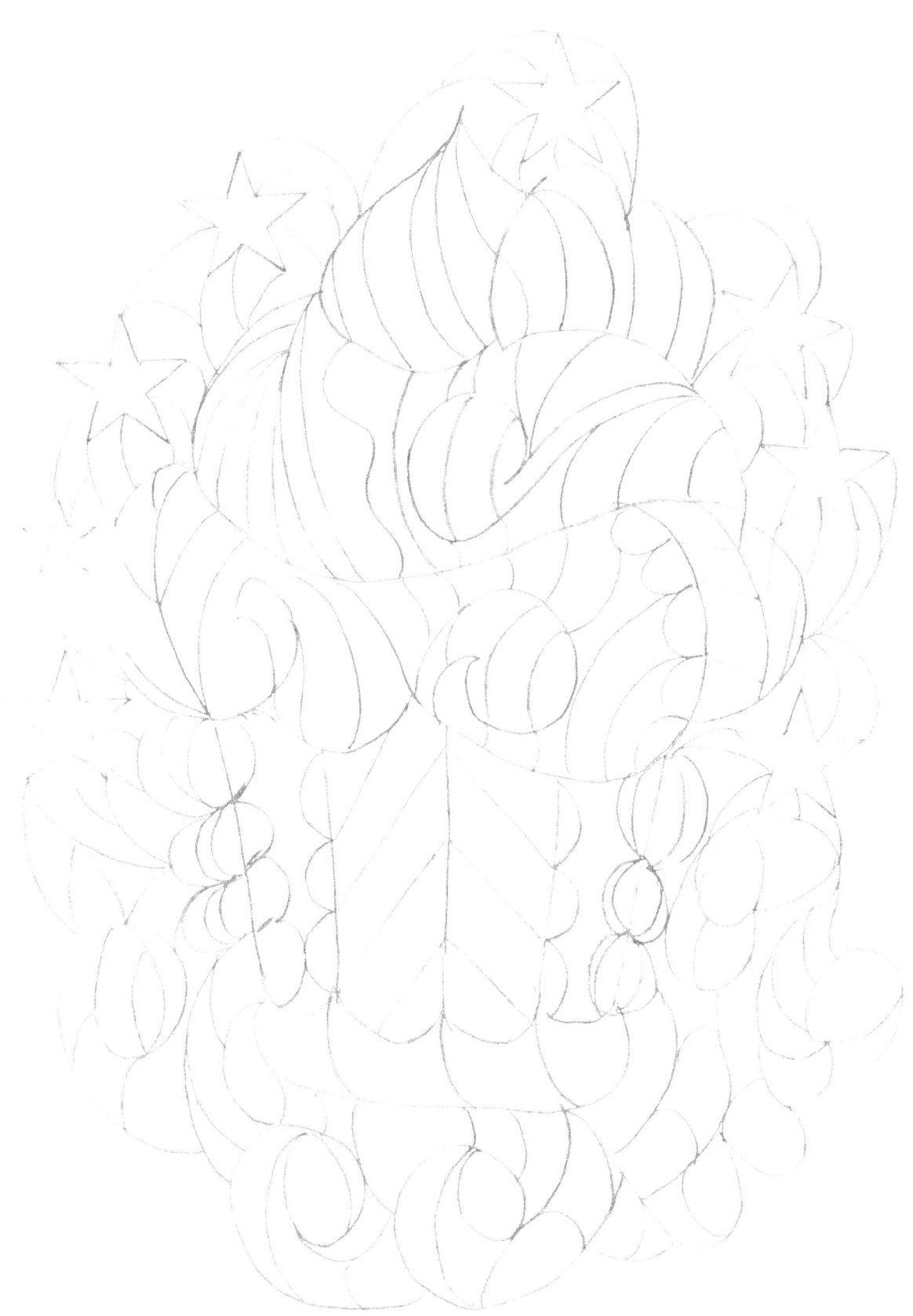

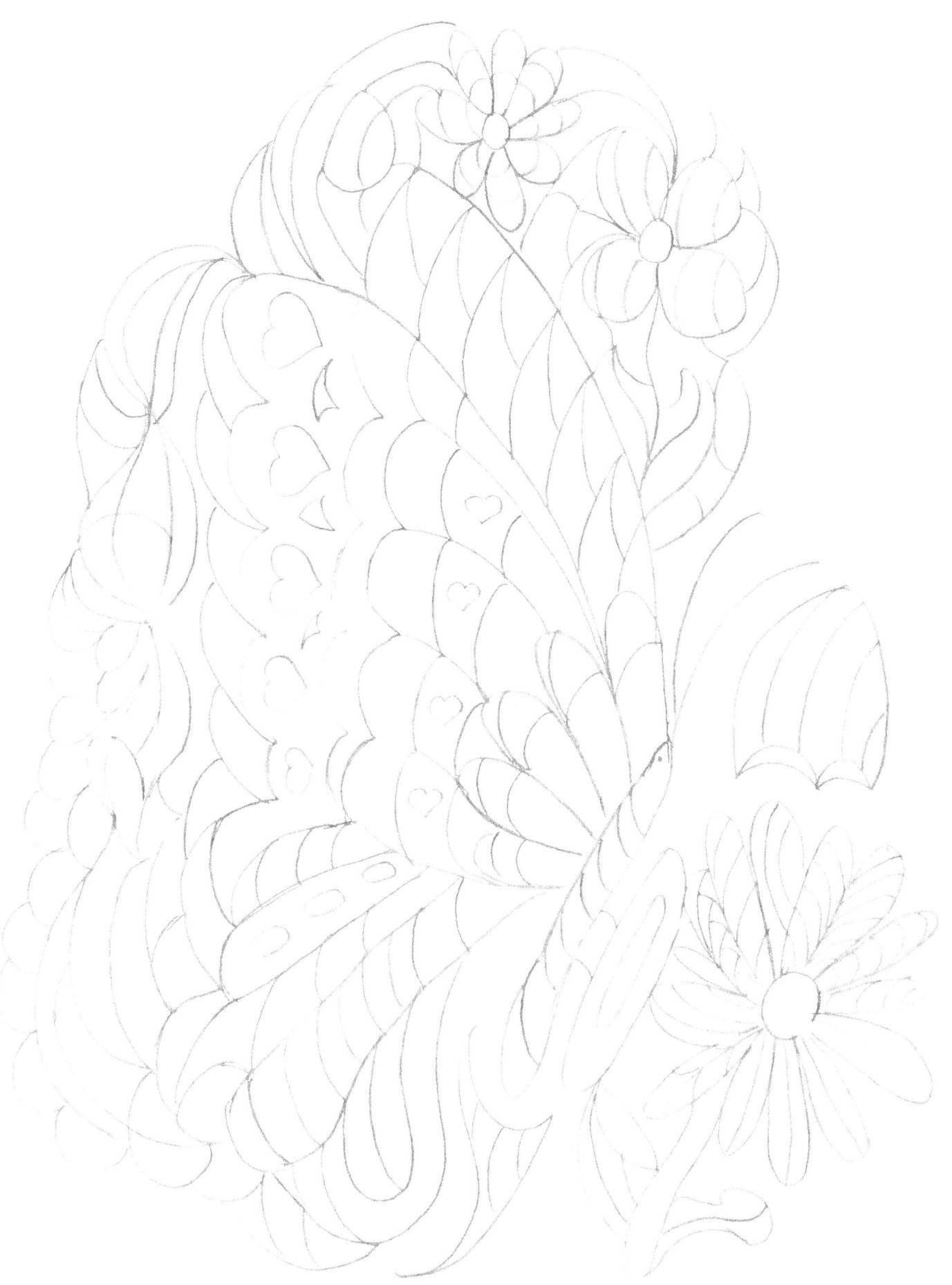

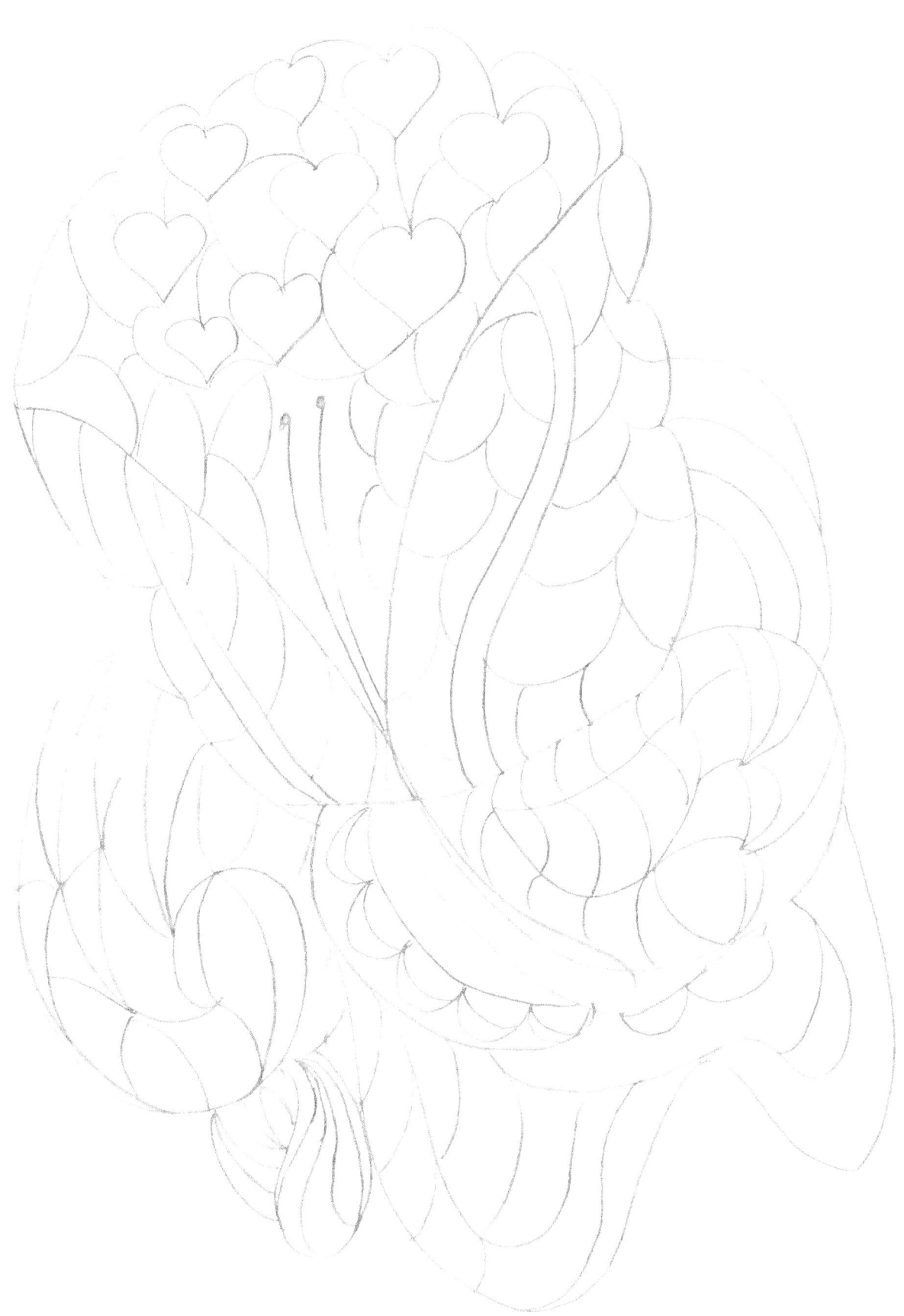

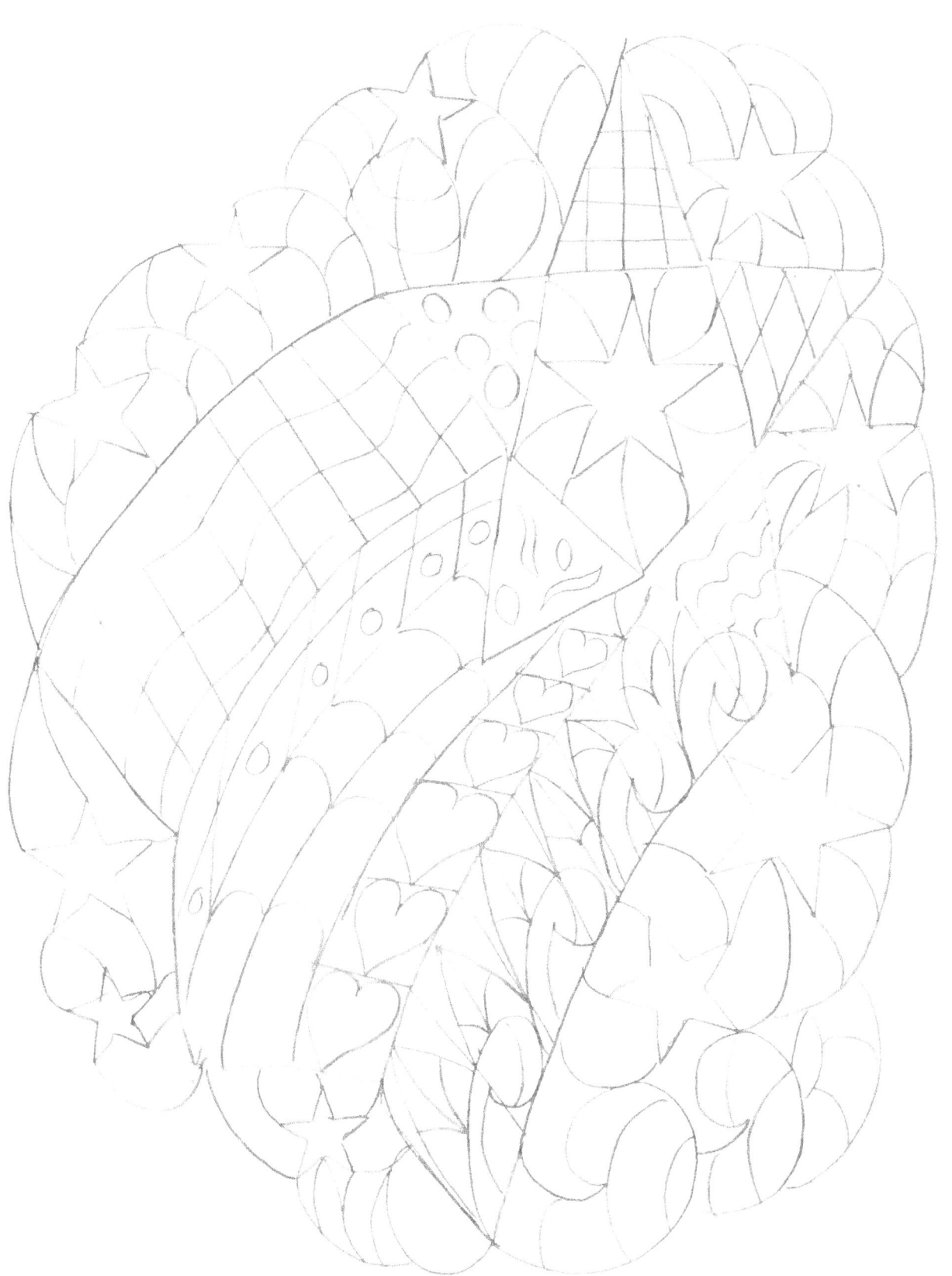

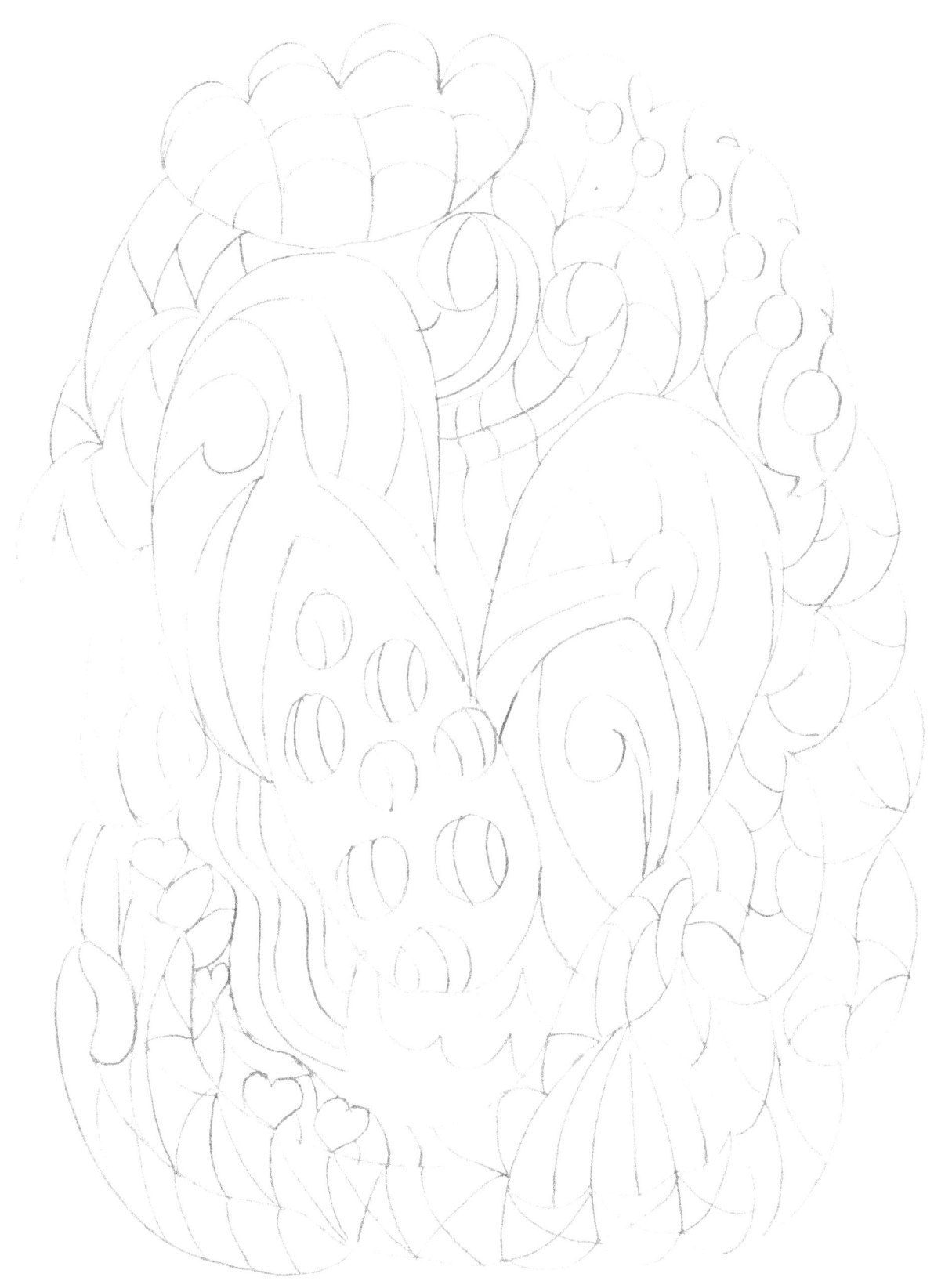

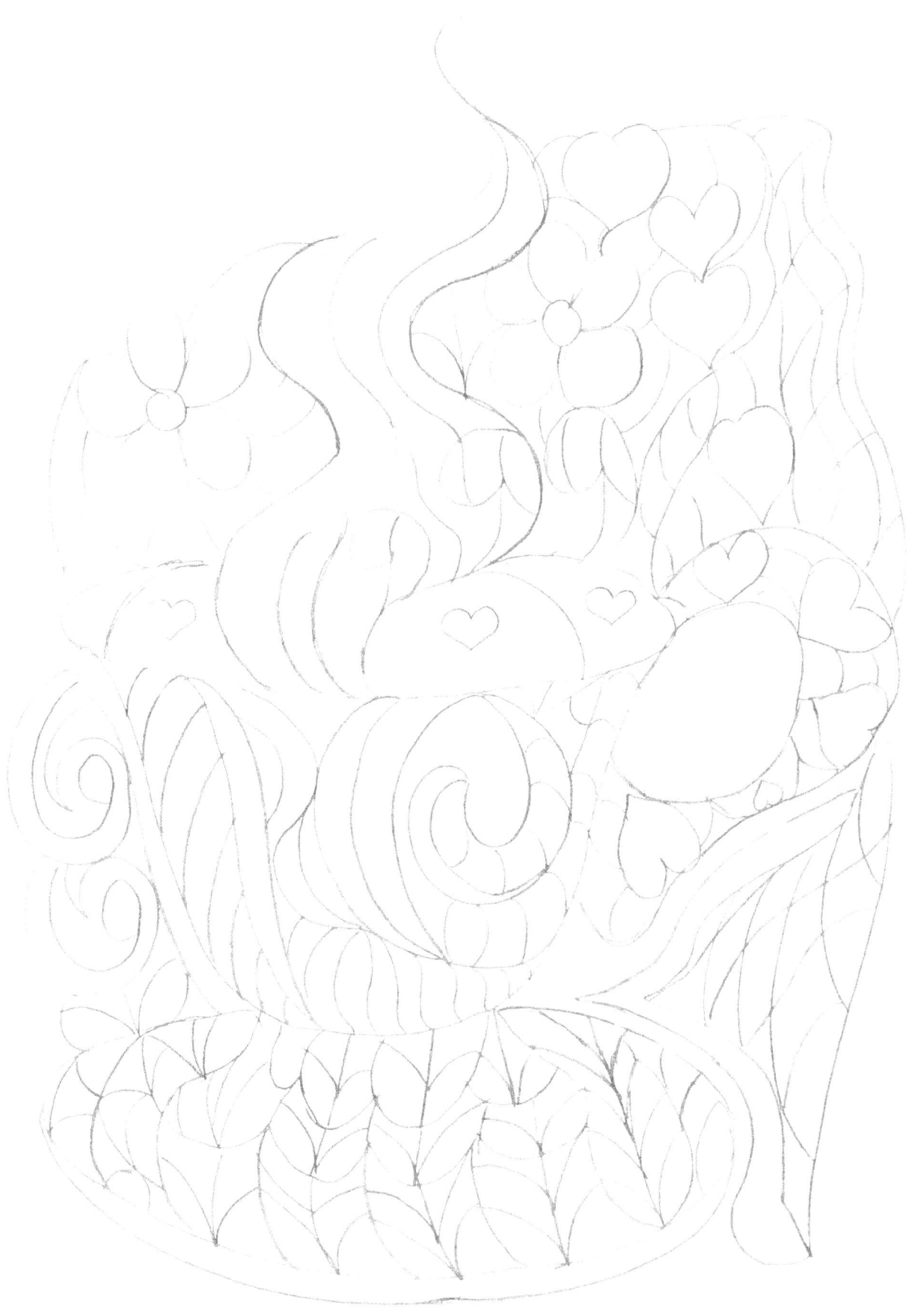